Walking Into Lightning

Walking Into Lightning

Ellen LaFlèche

Saddle Road Press

Saddle Road Press
Hilo, Hawai'i
saddleroadpress.com

Book design and cover photograph by Don Mitchell

ISBN 978-1-7329521-2-6
Library of Congress Control Number: 2019942229

.

Dedicated to

my beloved husband, the late John Patrick Clobridge

my beloved daughter and son-in-law Céline and Jeremy Vienneau

my beloved grandsons Jackson and Zachary Vienneau

and all families coping with neurological illnesses, especially ALS

Contents

NIGHT THUNDER BREAKING AGAINST A CANYON

COME NOW, AND

Come now, and feel the awe.
The heron is rising
into twilight like a prayer.
Hear
its psalm, the slow
mindful
beat of its flight.

Come now, and contemplate the joy of play.
See the sun and moon rocking
on their celestial seesaw.
The sun drifts down slow
as the moon floats up.

Come now, and inhale the incense.
Farmers have set their sugar cane fields on fire.
Feel the smoke spreading over the bayou in white spirals
fragrant as frangipani sticks.

Come now, and imagine.
Under the gray dreadlocks
of Spanish moss
a couple is falling into a frenzy
of love.
Listen to
the sweet Cajun cadence in their cries.

Come now, and accept the inevitable.
A bobcat is rippling toward the wild
boar roasting on a spit.

Come now, and ponder.
If everything happens for a reason
would you let the diamondback snake
coil its rattling bracelet around your wrist?

Come now, and dance.
Behind the juke joint
old musicians are slapping their thighs
and making the spoons and
fiddles sing.

Come now, and feel the awe.
The sun has set down
its crimson prayer blanket.
The heron has begun its descent,
floating through currents of mist,
landing on its feet with an angel's bodiless
grace.

THE SCENT OF YOUR NAPE WAS AUTUMN

Because the Dead Cannot Tell Us What It's Like to Die

That time our yard was a blurred gyroscope of snow
and our driveway a gloss lake of ice.
Your breath: a momentary ghost on our bedroom window.
Snow shivered the pine needles
and a maple branch snapped off at the elbow.
A blue jay slung a blur of sky across the storm
and somehow, somehow
the sun slipped through that momentary blueness.
Your breath on the glass glowed hot with light.
Dying might be like that.

That time we watched the ocean roll, ancient with salt,
with boneless creatures bobbing through the breakers.
The sun lulled our muscles like a hot stone massage.
The waves unfurled their bolts of lace
and you peered into a quahog's pink-lined jewel box.
Sunset turned the water to Sauvignon wine
and sailboats to palettes of van Gogh mauve.
But you said there was nothing so beautiful
as my long white hair lifting into a squall.
Dying might be like that.

That time in the shower
when you slid an oval of jasmine soap down my right arm,
then my left.
I slid the mauve oval down your left leg,
then your right.
Our breaths added the smell of fermented grapes
to the gathering mist. After the lathering,
steam lifted off your shoulders like a departing spirit.
My eyes wept away the soap's jasmine burn
and for a moment I saw you pass through the frosted glass door.
Dying might be like that.

BEFORE THE SICKNESS, WHEN

your hair was oak-leaf smoke on our pillow
and even in deepest June the scent of your nape was autumn
(mown hay, sweet corn turning to sugar in the fields)

before the sickness, when
your mouth was peach cider simmering in a dented sauce pan
the scent of your breath was plowed earth and cedar mulch
and your forehead sweat anointed my eyelids with sacramental oil

before the sickness, when
your strong back suppled against my palms
your spinal discs trembled like ivory wind chimes
and afterwards, in the shower,
I soaped the gentle jut of your shoulder blades
you washed the delicate skulls of my knees
and I licked the jasmine-scented suds that exploded against your nape

after the sickness, when
beneath that fragrant nape your nerve cells withered on their spinal vine

FEAR, THAT GOOD HALLUCINOGEN

after your diagnosis, we walk the shoreline in late July

Black clouds evocative as Rorschach blots.
I see something witchy in the ink—
swirl of robe, handle of broom.
A cauldron bulging with brews that could cure you.

Thunder prowls the west,
a fanged animal growling for the kill.

The ocean is all foaming smoke and hissing cinders.
A mermaid leans over the prow of a wave,
ghost nets shawled around her shoulders.

Lightning tasers the surf.
The Atlantic splits in fiery half.

You glow in lightning's X-ray chamber.
I see your irradiated face bones—
the animal trap of your jawline,
the twin knives of your cheeks.

You see my winged pelvis,
that good guardian angel.
You kneel on a carpet of kelp
and take that seraph into your arms.

CORN SENSORIUM

I took you this morning deep into August corn.
Bees hot with pollen hovered in place,
a chorus of humming harmonicas.
The air was slick with the scent of buried manure,
the distant tang of autumn apples.
When you said you could taste the apples in your lungs
we forgot (for a moment) your illness.

Deep into the maize
the air turned the gloomy muted green of a fairy tale forest,
the kind of forest where the owl swivels its horned head
to watch a yellow braid slither down the tower wall,
swivels its head in the other direction
to watch seven small men slouch toward the copper mine.

When you kissed me on the mouth
the maize became a maze, an emerald labyrinth,
and we wandered in spiraling loops. A break
in the clouds lit the stalks like medieval torches
and you saw the way out. Just before noon
we emerged on the opposite side of the field.

We carried home a basket filled with corn,
those shrunken mummies with skin-tight wrappings
and withered hairs. You boiled water in a copper pot,
softened a hunk of butter with a fork.

The kernels were ingots of carat gold
but a green worm dropped from the cob in my hand.

Dream (I)

Sometimes a dream snake is just a snake,
a water moccasin flashing through the brain's nocturnal swamp.
A rattle rattling in a newborn's hand.
Just a cobra, un-tranced,
collapsing into its cerebral basket.
A python winding like a caduceus around my beloved's spine.

WE REMINISCE ABOUT OUR FIRST WINTER SOLSTICE

Oh, the slow blizzard that night—
how white wings of snow
spiraled around the street lamp,
a languorous gathering of winter moths.

We walked in circles through the blizzard.
Snow drops dissolved on your tongue
like a newborn's memory of milk.
I was the angel maker—
dropping into snow, staring at the sky
where the solstice moon should have been glowing.
My limbs carved fragile wings in the drifts.

Remember the slow fire you stoked for us—
how you knelt in front of the fireplace
and stroked the log into a star-rush of sparks,
how the flames braided themselves into a twilled basket
that you filled with kindling?

Remember our unhurried love—
how you gave pleasure to my wrists,
my elbows, my ribcage?
On the longest night of the year I had time to love your face,
to tender your brow with my fingers.

Your eyelash was a slash of moon on my thumb.

After the Sickness Takes Away Your Sense of Smell

You sit in the breakfast nook
and watch the scent of autumn—
oak-leaf smoke curling from the neighbor's burning mound
mist rising from the basket of apples on our lawn
espresso beans whirring in the coffee grinder.

You open the woodstove door
and listen to the scent of winter—
kindling crackling like blistered bones
bark shriveling with the slow curl of a love letter
flames boring into the log like a deep tissue massage.

You walk barefoot into thunder
and feel the scent of spring—
ozoned air tingling the hairs on your arms
wet violets sliding against the soles of your feet
cold mud squelching against your heels.

After the sickness takes away your sense of smell
you press your knees against mine
and taste the scent of summer—
sweat and estrogen thickening under our sheet
my night breath in your mouth
the memory of cinnabar perfume on my wrists.

TODAY YOU TALK ABOUT FIRE

Those blue sparks when your steel-headed sperm
struck my ovum's spinning flint wheel.
How my ovaries glowed in the dark like clocks
with radium dials. Chemicals lit the fallopian tunnels
and my womb heated up, plush with blood. Our daughter
smoldered for months in my bed of uterine tinder.

That time we walked the shoreline at sunset
and the tide advanced in slow red ripples of fire.
We let it lick our feet, splash our ankles
and shins. When foam salt-stung my knees
I ran shrieking from the waves
but you dove into the hiss.

That April morning when we burned leaves
just to remember the autumn. Smoke
infused our hair with the scent of November.
You tossed chemicals into the blaze—
phosphorus to make the flames rage neon green,
potassium for a furious purple.

Today you talk about fire.
How a flame is a not a tongue
but a holy spirit hovering above a dying man's head.

Yesterday, X-rays crackled against your cranium.
Your nerves burned along the long fuse of your spine.

Today you talk about fire.
Should you melt into the slow heat of bodily rot
or the swift burn of cremation?

Today you say you love me.
My eggs are too old to ignite
but you kiss me all over,
your tongue a miracle of heat on my skin.

WE VISIT THE CEMETERY WHERE YOU MIGHT BE BURIED

Twin willows flank the wrought iron gates.
Dante-esque, but we enter:
the weeping begins here.

Here the dead are tucked into their lairs,
safe from hail, thunder, sorrow,
the scavenger's bone-gnaw and clawing.

We pass the stone angel with her face in her hands,
pass the cherub with his pouty mouth and fractured wings.

We pass the windowless crypt—
winter's storehouse of corpses.
It can't be true, it can't,
but I hear a creaking,
see the wooden door shiver on its hinges.

We find your Irish grandmother, five decades gone she is,
her headstone warm as bread against our palms.
I can't help wonder—
how long did Brigid's red hair flame in the grave?

She's dead beyond prayers, you say,
but you kneel anyway, your face in your hands.

Five steps down
we enter the next level of the dead.
A whitewashed chapel, willows fringing a pond so blue
there must be indigo dye in the water.
Monogamous swans swim infinite loops.

We walk among the pre-paid plots,
the gravestones spaced in perfect rows like dominoes.
The lawn is groomed to your ancestral green,
pampered with rake, blade, sprinkler.

A metal sign is nailed to a tree.

No Pets. No Picnics. No Teddy Bears.
Flowerpots Removed The First Of Every Month.

Your cane stabs the grass.
Forget this place, you say. *I'd rather be cremated.*

PRAYER FOR DESPAIR

Because the full moon is trembling inside its executioner's hood, because
a human foot can be molded into a putrefying lotus, because
the tantric beauty of a dragonfly pleasuring the river's skin.

Because pine sap is the smell of coffin planks being sawed, because
a pit viper exchanges venomous spit with its lover, because
corn plants are rattling their cobs like Zuni rain dancers.

Because I bloom in your mouth like a carved radish in water.

Because the sun is slicing the horizon's spine like a circular saw, because
double-headed trout are swimming through irradiated water, because
the unkissable beauty of fire.

Because a loaded gun feels warm as flesh in its holster, because
the amaryllis flower sits on its stalk like a peeled-back brain, because
the aromatic beauty of lilacs drooping like milk-filled breasts.

Because a house is groaning under fire's fury, because
a shackled man is begging his captor for a kiss of water, because
oak leaves are lurching through autumn like sun-stunned bats.

Because soon you will hold a bouquet of flames to your chest.

NORTH INTO FIRE

our last road trip before you enter home hospice

I drive us into Vermont's cyclical incineration.
The foliage makes this sound:
bracelets of brass bells tingling a woman's wrist,
and this:
a psalm for mercy on a supplicant's lips.

Leaves twist through the pre-evening breeze.
In slow layers they drift,
calm as snow but vivid—
the good maroon of birth,
of throbbing cord blood.

You crave a splash of blue in the maples.
Not the sky slipping through foliage,
not that hue, not the shined blue
of a mussel glossed by sun and sea water.

We find a village too small to appear
on the map. A place where pumpkins loll in the fields
like corpulent pigs, where a lake sits serene as a mirror.
A duck shivers silt from its feathers.
Its head is green as a horsefly's head
but the lake is almost the blue you crave.

The foliage makes this sound:
a woman in a silk dress brushing static through her hair
and this:
an ancient bible rustling in a scholar's gloved hand.

We reminisce about the autumn we were newlyweds,
the leaves so brittle with drought they sounded like rain
when they fell. We raked them into mounds
and rolled in them,
rolled until we were breaded,
and breathless.

Back home, fire hasn't reached us yet.
Our maple tree makes this sound:
soft applause after a Schumann symphony,
and this:
the long sad sigh of a blood pressure cuff.

A blue jay flits through the branches. *This,* you say.
This. This is the blue you crave.

I REFUSE TO READ THE *DEATH WITH DIGNITY* BROCHURE

Hard enough this work of dying—
when eyes ascend into skull like angels into sky,
sockets gone blind, white as soft-boiled albumin.

Hard enough this work of dying—
when plugged lungs crave a sip of oxygen,
chest muscles taut with the strain of exhaling.

Hard enough this work of dying—
when pain levitates you like an exorcism
then slams you back down.

I feel your soul detaching from your body,
a wrenching ache like tendons pulled slow from bone.

I hear you rasp:
Don't tranquilize me when I start to thrash.

Love,
ride the hospital bed like a mechanical bull.
Fling the cards and flowers from your tray.
Roll your head like a revolving fan.
Spit out the butterscotch pudding, the puréed peas.
Shit and piss and flail. Refuse
the bedpan, the hairbrush, the needle.
Curse this dying, curse it to hell,
wail all night, wail.

Watch me throw *Death with Dignity* into the fireplace flames.

QUIETLY

Early evening.
The sun looms on the horizon like a rogue
planet knocked out of its orbit.
The sheets I left on the line crackle under its shadow.

I remember when you burned the leaves we had raked,
cupping the match like a monk who has cloaked himself in gasoline.

Did the monk sit quietly when the lit match crackled against his ribs?

You sat quietly when the doctor said you were going to die.
Maybe a tremble in the hollow of your throat,
a shiver of your downturned palms.

The cold scrape of your chair against the hardwood floor.

You were a man in a white gown patterned with violets and hearts.
A rogue shadow sat on top of your X-rayed spine.

Did the monk hold his breath against
the fire whooshing into his lungs?
You try to hold your breath but the mask makes you breathe,
it makes you breathe.

The smell of burning leaves is a violet haze on the edge of town.
Smoke bruises the sickbed sheets on our line.

The blue of this pre-dusk sky has settled in your limbs,
the slow curve of your jaw.

The sun drops quietly into the mountainous west.

Because You Love the Desert, May Your Death

be easy as drifting into the arms of a cactus
razored clean of its needles,
the nubs on its skin sensuous against your cheek
as the warm bumps that circle a woman's nipple.

May your feet, blueing as they cool, turn to mist
on the desert floor. May the Sonoran stars
arrange themselves like the notes in your vintage songbook.
Ella. Etta. Nina. Lena.

When the rattlesnake shivers its maraca
may your rising spirit rumba

to its rhythm. May the cactus
bloom in the night like a moon-flower plant,
petals enfolding your spirit in a luminous shroud.

May the white coyote, her belly bulging with pups,
circle around your body, circling and circling,
panting mist from her lungs.

May the coyote kneel with her paws on your chest.
May she toss back her head,
fanging the Navajo moon,
keening and keening the loss of you.

Blessing for an Imminent Death

Because my husband is strumming the bed rails
(this music of the almost dead), because
his heart is saxophoning a ragged jazz beat, because
his wide-mouthed gasps are jagged as sex breaths,
let there be dance.

Because the brass urn yearns for his burned laughter, his fatless ash,
mercy.

Because his sheets are sticky wet with almost-death, because
water hangs in crystal baubles from our daughter's eyelids, because
the visiting nurse enters your room without knocking,
sorrow.

Because my husband is strumming the bed rails
(this stringed requiem of the almost dead), because
his feet are blue-hued fetuses in my palms, because
the riffling of his lungs is soft as flamenco fans unfolding,
let there be psalms.

Because tufts of snow are nippling our pine trees, because
his skin is releasing the scent of sugar fields burning, because
my thumbs are stroking the blunted blades of his cheekbones,
let there be grace.

Because candle flames are swaying like an ecstatic choir, because
my husband is strumming the bed rails
(this eerie symphony of the almost dead), because
clouds are flying across the moon like a gathering of spirits,
let there be death.

Because the brass urn yearns for him with uterine ferocity,
let there be life.

AFTER

I unwrap a slab of soap scented with honey and milk
after I dip the washcloth in water so hot
it could make a living person shiver
as if the steam that scalds my hands
could unstiffen his limbs, could re-warm his bones,
could make him sit up in bed with the biblical grace of the risen

after I wash his eyelids, his lips, his temples,
after I dip my finger in the small font at the end of his spine
after I bathe him between his thighs
as if he could feel soap suds bursting against his glans

after I kneel by his bed
and dry his feet with my hair

I pick up the phone
and make the calls.

I COULD PULL THAT SOUL FROM ITS RIVER

STILL LIFE

On my table,
sympathy gifts in the perfect asymmetry
of a still life watercolor:
a bouquet of roses rubbed raw of thorns,
green carnations in a ribboned box. Blood
oranges in a pewter bowl.
When did I open the door to an artist?

My neighbor adds a jug of wine to the canvas,
a pair of silver goblets. A box of Anjou pears—
fertile goddesses in wax-paper robes.

The coffee maker bull-snorts steam from its nostrils.
Oolong brews to amber in a glass carafe.
Fingers place something round and white on my tongue.
When did I open the door to a priest?

Outside the picture window
a winter landscape in watercolor:
Pyrrol Orange, Burnt Scarlet.
Sunset is a raging chimney fire,
clouds smoking like creosote-soaked rags.
The flames crackle in my head.

The priest steals a blood orange from the still life
tableau, peels it in a way too slow
for a new widow to bear. Red nectar
stains his thumb and forefinger.

A stranger carries my husband's suit on a hanger.
When did I open the door to the undertaker?

My maple tree shivers in the wind. Branches
dance around each other like battling shadows.

Night enters sideways—
a hearse's curtains sliding shut.

Because You Loved the Ocean

I hope your death was a warm tide rolling you into the salt.

When sea foam fizzed against your skin
I hope you remembered those nights when my fingertips
electrified your spine, your cheekbones,
the soles of your feet.

I hope a sea wave carried you on its back
and you drifted gentle into the deep.
I hope a choir of buoys chanted their low-toned dirge
and a humpback whale soothed you with its ancient throat song.

I hope a galaxy of starfish whirled beneath you
and an angelfish pressed her lush mouth against your final breath.

When sunset swirled its watercolors through pearlescent clouds
and waves tossed your body high above the water
I hope you rose into paradise
with a halo of luminescing plankton above your head
and a star in your hand.

After the Memorial Service, I Pour Myself a Cup of Tea

Steamed aromas dampen my hair:
tannin, oolong leaves, a whisper of earth. My fortune
dangles, a wet kite wobbling on its Lipton string.

The teabag billows out,
the skirt of a woman drowning herself in a river.

> The river woman must have held her breath,
> pebbles rune smooth under her soles,
> pearl necklace floating on the water like a string of buoys.

I take no pleasure in the clink of bone
china on bone china, in the silver tongs
vibrating my cup's rim with tuning fork precision.

> The woman's lungs must have filled with river,
> with its stirred-up muck, its sodden leaves.

I filter boiling oolong through my teeth. My tongue
accepts the searing. Droplets roll back into the cup,
black as mascara-stained tears.

> When the woman drank river did she remember her lover,
> the underside of his wrist, the scoop of his pelvic bone-boat?

My teabag bulges, a woman's soul bloated with sin.
I could pull that soul from its river,
set it dripping on my floral saucer.

But I let those sins rupture into my cup.

> Did she remember his warm mouth kissing her throat,
> his cool palm soothing her migrained head?

Once I spat your kiss from my mouth.
Twice I pushed away your hand.
Many times I turned from your gaze.

Sip by sip, I drink my sins.

Anecdotes I Didn't Share at Your Memorial Service

How the night before our first Thanksgiving
we lit each other instead of apple spice candles.
Autumn's tang scented our limbs,
the sun-dried sheets. You didn't make a sound
but I cried out as I melted. When your calf muscles
began their slow trembling
you held my shoulders to rudder yourself.

> How a month before you died
> you craved the color blue as if sky and jay
> weren't enough. I rubbed skeins of indigo
> yarn against the rough grain of your arm hairs.
> I told you to imagine our hydrangea bush
> pushing blue blossoms through the snow
> that blew in undulating drifts against our window.

How the day after our third Thanksgiving
I felt the twinge of my egg hurled like a new world
out of God's ovarian fist. Gravity
yanked it downward,
spun it through my fallopian tunnel.
Your comet drilled through the crust,
bored down to the planetary core. Stunned,
our daughter bubbled into life.

> How a week before you died
> you couldn't swallow but still
> you craved the taste of yellow.
> I touched a slice of lemon to your tongue,
> ran a buttered corn cob against your lips.
> January sun was a slab of yolk on the sickroom wall.

How the night our daughter was born
the cervical slit had to widen into an astonished
stare. My hips shifted, creaking as they softened.
When I rode the rattling gurney to the birth room
you sang to me. You sang.
When our daughter swam
head first out of her amniotic cove,
you sang to her. You sang.

      How the day before you died
      you craved the sound of green.
      I rubbed a jade brush against my scalp until
      my long hair crackled
      and danced. I played Schumann's
      Spring Symphony on our vintage turntable.
      The vinyl crackled like buckled lungs.
      You kept time by blinking, blinking.
      Our daughter sang to you. She sang.

WALKING INTO LIGHTNING

Because my husband loved the thunder

I walk into lightning with a metal urn in my hands.

The wind witches my black skirt around my ankles.
A boom shivers my rose bush,
lifts its root ball half out of the grave.

Static crackles my scalp.
I smell wet earth and whirling pine needles.
Electrified lilacs.

When I hear that growl like a dropped bomb
just before it whistles
and the sky throbs against my retina like an ocular migraine
I decant him into the storm.

Ashes drift through my hair.
A bone shard punctures my boot.

I blow a billow of him off my palm.

LAMENTATION FOR THE 99TH DAY WITHOUT YOU

Because I remember luring you into a forest of corn.
How the sun lit a thesaurus of greens on the stalks.
Our mouths emitted a glossary of love sounds.
Hair drifted in scorched brown strands from the cobs.

Because I remember rowing with you in the ocean.
My earrings bobbed in currents of wind like silver fishing lures.
I don't remember the sunset that stained the waves to a bloody froth.

After the diagnosis,
mourning doves settled deep in the fragrance of lilacs.

Rain rippled our bedroom window like a beaded curtain.
Your leg muscles raged against the withering:
ripple and release, ripple and release.
The rippling in your thighs looked like love but it hurt.
You said that it hurt.

Because I remember the clack of my black high heels
climbing the funeral home steps.
I wore a silk slip under my plain brown dress.
Leaning into your coffin rubbed a small bliss against my calves.

I don't remember descending the funeral home steps.
I remember the twelve-footed march of the pall bearers,
the hearse opening its doors like an industrial oven.

I drove home through a canopy of maples.
I saw sorrow on the telephone wires: a lamentation of doves.

My bedroom window is dark as the wrong side of a mirror.
Tomorrow will be 100 days without you.

Prayer for the Newlywed Couple Who Bought Our House After You Died

The bride, Miriam. Bless her still
redolent with the scent of honeymoon,
her face scraped raw by stubble,
the soles of her feet pumiced smooth
by her bridegroom's tongue.

The groom, Josiah. Bless him burning smudge sticks
in the kitchen. Let the sweet smoke disperse
the lingering molecules of meals we once cooked.
The ghost-smells of corned beef and cabbage,
of fried eggs and melting ham fat,
let them drift out the window on ribbons of vaporized sage.

Bless Miriam hanging lace curtains in the dining room. Praise
the evening sun leaking its smudged smoke through the fabric.
Praise the lightness of lace, praise it falling
and rising, falling and rising, for that lace is filling
its lungs with evening breeze.

Let Josiah be tender when he rips
seagreen tiles from the bathroom floor,
for our hair and skin cells are sealed under the grout.
May he discard our DNA with appropriate awe.

Bless Miriam stripping roses off our bedroom walls,
those pink blossoms wilting in her hands.
Praise the reek of wallpaper glue and crumbling plaster.

Bless the spontaneous lovemaking in the herb garden.
Praise Miriam, the scent of sage in her hair and crushed mint
on her fingers. Praise the unbearable tenderness
of the groom as he kisses his bride.

PRAYER FOR WEEPING

Because the white coyote is howling mist from its lungs, because
ice entombs the night-seeking roots of the moonflower, because
a woman is licking winter from her lover's nape, because
the cruel beauty of a lumberjack's hand on a steaming tree stump.

Because a lover is brushing salt from a woman's scalp, because
my uterus is sweating blood at the memory of love, because
a child is ripping a littleneck clam from its shell, because
the communal beauty of a bridal veil being lifted.

Because the moon is grimacing like a mouth in rigor, because
a hunchbacked man is pruning his rose garden, because
once a lover slickened that hump with patchouli oil, because
the kissable beauty of an angelfish mouth.

Because my eyes are salivating with the memory of mauve, because
a rose takes weeks to bloom on the lacemaker's needle, because
the scent of burning amber is the scent of coming, because
the breakable beauty of a hyoid bone.

Because autumn's bloodbath is spreading across my lawn, because
a weeping willow is dancing hula just before a storm, because
my mouth is weeping at the memory of kissing, because
the redundant beauty of blizzard on a cold white gravestone.

Dream (II)

We lie down together, twining like seaweed where the ocean
scours the bony rock of earth.

The moon glows blue-green above us,
a bloom of tidal plankton.

The wind rubs salt against my skin
and I remember you died.
Kneeling, you watch the slow
doleful tolling of my hips.

The buoys lean forward as if in prayer.

Your gaze pulls sweat from my pores
and I become more water
than flesh, phosphorescent as the sea's glowing wake.

Dusk merges into night. Stars emerge,
sparking like the static pulses of a woman
brushing her hair in winter.

You dive, sea-mammaling into my waves
and when you come up for air
I pull you under, and under again.

I arrange your body on the sand.
Night merges into mourning
and you are all seaweed hair and salt-baked bones.

Your spine detaches,
rides the tidal surge like a sea horse.
Your toe bones walk the shoreline.

I pick up your knee bones. I lift them slowly over my head,
double skulls filled with ritual wine.
And I drink.

THE STAGES OF LOSS

Say your neighbor's snake slinks out of its cage,
oozing like pudding through a seam in the glass.
You wait all night for the slither beneath the covers,
the spray of venomous spit. And say just before morning
you dream the cobra's face swaying above yours,
a slow, sinuous lover.
Fear is like that.

Say you have a meeting with the undertaker
and the waiting room looks like a bridal suite—
white walls, white drapes, white roses in a milk glass vase.
And say that you hear a sudden grief-cry,
a woman's sharp *ohhh.*
Sorrow is like that.

Say the police search your house for the cobra.
They use a pole to lift your shirts off their hangers.
They turn your pant legs inside out.
They peer into your oven like Gretel's witch.
Say there's no sign of your serpentine dream lover.
You breathe relief from your lungs.
Denial is like that.

Say the undertaker keeps you waiting.
You wait and wait.
And say a woman emerges from his office,
eyes lush with tears,
her hair spiking wild as lightning from its bun.
You stare at her. You stare and stare.
And say that when the undertaker ushers you
into the casket room
you can't help fingering the white satin lining.
The undertaker stands quietly,
hands clasped at his waist in solidarity with the dead.
Rage is like that.

Say you are doing laundry
and the cobra emerges like an umbilical cord
from the watery belly of your washing machine.
Its eyes stare into yours, a kind of feral longing.
You stare back. You stare and stare.
And say the snake slides into the laundry basket,
sinking with a slow reptilian shiver into your sheets.
Acceptance is like that.

LAMENTATION FOR THE 199TH DAY WITHOUT YOU

That time at the ocean when white sand gritted my vision.
Seagulls hovered like crosses over the waning tides.
A pelican veered from its squadron,
a dozen fish stacked in its pouch like a payload of bombs.

The sun poured its hot wax across your back,
the underside of your elbows.
I rubbed sunscreen on your shoulders,
kissed the salted hollow just above your spine.
You turned, eyes gazing to heaven.
And burned to ruddy splendor.

I remember stroking your cold cremains.
Remnants of elbow and hip, a curve of skull.
Shards so sharp they could have slivered under my skin.

You were the odorless dead. No scent of baked bone
or roasted tendon. The dank fog of your armpits—
gone.

I remember between your thighs there was lemon grass,
an elegantly carved peace pagoda.
Once my fingers walked that holy ground,
strolling like pilgrims under the pagoda's holy shadow.

Tomorrow will be 200 days without you.

NIGHT THUNDER BREAKING AGAINST A CANYON

CREDO FOR THINGS THAT CRACK AND BREAK

I believe in night thunder breaking against a canyon.
Hail that cracks open a peony's skull.
Lightning that splits and splits itself,
a cell in swift mitosis.

I believe that dawn does not crack or break,
no. Dawn is a languid unfurl,
a woman releasing hair pin by pin from her nape.

I believe in river ice cracking against rock:
the tectonic moans of a woman laboring in stirrups.

I remember breakfast at the Crack O' Dawn Café.
How the cook broke our eggs with his knuckles,
how stuffing leaked from the booth's cracked vinyl skin.

I believe hearts never break,
but when they do
they crack into shards like a biblical vessel in the shape of a woman.

Last night I dreamed you released opalized strands from my braid.
I woke to first light spreading across my pillow. That dawn,
that breaking.

I believe in DNA breaking apart for love.
We made sounds like river ice cracking against rock.
That slow genetic dance,
your chromosomes twisting around mine,
mine against yours.

I believe spirits cannot be broken,
but when they break
the sun is a blind spot on the sky's tender retina.
That sudden nightfall.

That dawn.

ALL SOULS

I remember our first Halloween together

How we walked through a forest of orange.
Wind lifted hair off my shoulders
and spun the leaves into pinwheels of fire.
I remember how you carried home a bouquet of foliage.
I don't remember the spider that crawled up your sleeve.

At home I displayed your bouquet in the fireplace.
Just before twilight our doorbell chimed.
You tossed apples to the ghost smoking through a hole in his sheet.
I gave chocolate kisses to a zombie bride.

That night you eased me from a dream,
finger-whisking my hair,
dipping your tongue in the hollow of my throat.
You smelled like wet wool and cider mill smoke.
I remember your Adam's apple bobbing against my lips.

I don't remember you stroking the soft goatee between my legs.
I remember my drowsy thighs opening
without knowing they were opening.
That was the night an ovum rose like a harvest moon
over my fallopian orchard.
I dreamed of a shy girl hiding under her placental veil.

In the morning a ghost costume skittered across our lawn.

I ACCEPT

that my wedding dress hangs in yellowing folds from a cellar rafter.
That cobwebs cover the bodice like an overlay of lace.
The cobweb-spinner is a widow,
burdened by time's red hourglass.

That mothballs fill my linen closet with the fust of aging.
That my bedroom smells like flannel nightgowns and Avon talc.
The Avon Lady is a widow,
tubes of lipstick staining her palm like blood-tipped bullets.

That my wedding dress shivers its hips to the lacemaker's touch.
That a pearl button droops above the zipper like a disc
slipped from its spine.
The dressmaker is a widow,
pins and threaded needles jutting from her teeth.

That my mirror cries and cries after my evening bath.
That my hair flings its tears into the fireplace flames.
The firetender is a widow,
ash and crackling sap singeing her broom.

That my wedding bouquet is powder and thorns in a cardboard box.
That the bouquet was seven white roses bound with ribbon and lace.
I am the grower of roses,
bags of bone meal stacked in the cellar,
my widowed fingers stung by thorns
and stung again.

LAMENTATION FOR THE 299TH DAY WITHOUT MY HUSBAND

I remember the dark coffee smell of his breath in my mouth,
the tea-tree taste of his hair in my teeth.

I can't remember the sound of his eyelids closing into love.

I remember him stepping out of a bath towel,
black hair spreading wet as ink on the pillow.
I can't remember the shape of his mouth,
the slow slant of jaw—
his face is vanishing into my brain's neuronal mist.

I remember when a vapor rose from our sheets,
how it smelled like earth and fish and peonies.

I remember him stepping out of the ocean with a star in his hand.

Our daughter tossed like an immigrant in my uterine hold.
Gardenia-scented milk flowed into her newborn mouth.
My husband thumb-rubbed my stretch marks,
luminous on my belly as folds of opalescent silk.

I don't remember his eyelids closing into death.
I remember our wedding night,
how I waltzed my groom under a teardrop chandelier.

Tomorrow will be 300 days without him.

UNBEARABLE

Remembering our honeymoon brings sorrow and joy

Unbearable, how the scent of gardenia
was almost too heavy to breathe. On the hotel veranda
we splurged on fine wine and watched sunset spread
its slow flush across evening's throat.

The waitress brought littleneck clams steaming in their own
salted broth. Unbearable,
how my groom picked the one with a fleshy nub
protruding from its smile. He dipped the soft meat in butter and

lifted it dripping to my mouth.
The clam belly slid like raw egg down my throat.

I tipped a shell against his lips and told him to drink.
Too sandy, he said, *too salty*, but he swallowed the broth,
wiping his beard with the knuckled swipes of a prehistoric man.

We clinked our wine glasses and watched the air move from
shadowed dusk to that deep blue moment just before
night. Unbearable, how the August moon,
engorged with heat,
dropped into the sea's labial waves.

In our suite
I smelled brine on his beard. Pin
by pin he released my hair from its bridal knot.

I untied his tie.

BENEDICTION FOR THE 364TH UNMARRIED DAY

Because the night before he died
the moon steamed like a woman rising out of a ritual bath.

Once his voice trembled the percussive skin of my eardrum.
Once I trembled the tender hairs on his nape.

I remember the comfort of Egyptian cotton sheets.
How we wrapped our winter selves in them,
double mummies luxuriating in our marital steam.

Because once I licked Jarrah honey from a wooden spoon.
Once he drilled his tongue into a lemon's yellow sting.

An hour before our daughter was born
he watched me surrender blood and water onto paper sheets.
He placed ice chips on my tongue.
I shivered as the baby steamed from my thighs.

I watched him shiver on deathbed sheets.
I fed him ice chips, morphine, lemon Jell-O.

Because the night before he died, I walked outside.
Stars swayed crazily in my tears.
I remembered paper lanterns strung like stars
across the veranda of our honeymoon hotel.

I grieved as a woman,
bending into his casket.
My womb tipped forward,
a long-necked urn spilling its ash.

I surrendered him to the thunder he loved.
His ashes shivered with each percussive rumble.
Lightning spidered down its electric thread.

Because the first time he lay with me,
I lit a lemon-scented candle.
He loved me wordlessly, soundlessly.
Breathlessly.

Tomorrow will be one year.

THE GRIEF EATER

*Vacation in a rented cottage during which I ponder the difference
between grieving and mourning*

I open another woman's curtains
and let dusk enter the kitchen. Tropical dusk,
scented with jasmine and magnolia,
an undernote of roses—dreamy musk
from another woman's garden.

My beloved died. He died. I don't have another.
Mourning is ritual—
black dress, black shawl, black shoes
heavy as wooden blocks on a woman's feet.

Grieving is interior—
a slow desire dream that shivers a woman from sleep.

My dinner simmers in a borrowed pot.
I'm making borscht,
that good root soup.

Mourning is a woman tossing rose petals into a fresh-dug pit.
Grieving is needles of novocaine numbing a heart.

I toss fresh herbs into the borscht and stir.
The swirls move outward, circular
ripples on the leafy surface of a pond. I stir
and stir, and the dusk is almost night,
a plum so ripe with summer
its flesh hemorrhages purple to black.

My beloved died. He died. I don't have another.

Mourning is death's ceremony—
a procession of villagers drumming toward the cemetery.
A raft drifting out to sea, wooden slats
crackling with fire and human ash.

I think I am done with mourning.

I bring the bowl of borscht to my lips.
Grief is a woman eating alone.

IN MEMORY OF OUR THIRD DATE

*While taking a walk after sunset we tried to identify the moment when
dusk becomes night*

When I saw the moon glow with the delicate
light of a paper lantern hanging over a banquet table,
I said *now*, this is *night*.

You said *no, not yet*. There's residual blue in the west,
a deep dusk-blue on the verge of onyx.

When we passed a house so incandescent with candlelight
it radiated like a soul from the inside out,
I said *now*.

No, you said, *not yet*. Only when the sky is sequined with stars
and mosquitoes have retreated with their bags of stolen blood,
only then is night.

When the dark rippling on Lily Bridge Lake melted into the hills
and perfume pulsed from the unfurling petals
of a moonflower garden, I said *now. This is night*.

You said *almost there*, and took my hand. We circled the lake,
listened to the wild flutter of wings we barely could see.

My eyes knew this absence of light. My pupils opened to darkness
slow as the gaze of a woman lying near her lover.

Now, you said, *now*.

PANTOUM FOR KISSING

in memory of our second date

If you kiss me, my mouth will open slow as birth
my breath will melt in your throat like snow falling on ocean
I will murmur like a prayer your beautiful name
your name in my mouth will shiver against my uvula

My breath will melt in your throat like snow falling on ocean
if you kiss me, you may take my long white hair in your fist
your name in my mouth will shiver against my uvula
my hair will spill like milk from your fist

If you kiss me, you may take my long white hair in your fist
I will sweat the scent of brine and sea wrack
my hair will spill like milk from your fist
my tongue on yours will soften to an edible petal

I will sweat the scent of brine and sea wrack
if you kiss me, you may murmur my beautiful name
my tongue on yours will soften to an edible petal
my name may roll like Parisian French in your throat

If you kiss me, you may murmur my beautiful name
I will gather delicious rose and hibiscus from my garden
my name may roll like Parisian French in your throat
you may sweat the scent of cedar and moss

I will gather delicious rose and hibiscus from my garden
if you kiss me, my mouth will open slow as birth
you may sweat the scent of cedar and moss
I will murmur like a prayer your beautiful name

BENEDICTION FOR THE LAST TIME WE KISSED

Because the first time we kissed
my hair moved slow as blackstrap syrup through your hands.

The last time we kissed
a nurse trimmed your beard and dressed you
in a simple white gown like a country bride.

Because the first time we kissed
I placed yellow tea roses in a cobalt vase.
Orchids in a fluted wine glass.

The last time we kissed
there were wilted carnations in a plastic jug.
Giftshop roses on a hospital tray.

Because the first time we kissed
I brought you chocolate croissants on a silver plate.

The last time we kissed
the IV bag hovered over your bed,
a goblin's bobbling head.

Because the first time we kissed
I tasted chocolate croissant on your tongue.

The last time we kissed
a nurse carried in vials and needles on a plastic tray.

Who knew a man's tongue could wither like the long muscle
of a leg, the striated muscle of a heart?
My husband's last kiss was slurred but it was slow,
it was slow.

BLINDFOLD

If I find a new beloved
let there be wild scallions lolling on the cutting board
raspberries weeping in the colander
basil leaves bleeding aromatic oils against my fingers.

Let me place a blue-scented candle on a circle of lace.
Let white clouds blindfold the moon
and my lace curtains blur the window like a pattern of frost.

Let me close my lover's fingers around a clove of garlic
and my lover drip Sauvignon wine on my tongue.
Let August wind carry insects that nibble and suck

and when a mosquito pushes into my nape
let there be a tender slap
and a smear of blood on my lover's palm.

Let the wild scallions languish on the cutting board.
Let the salmon scorch to black in the pan
and garlic bulbs soften like hearts in the salmon's ash.

Let my lover's white hair taste like milk and thunder in my mouth.
Let our limbs move in the slow spirals of synchronized swimmers
and my long white hair
fall like a blindfold over my new lover's eyes.

Dying might be like that.

Notes and Acknowledgments

ALS, also known as Lou Gehrig's disease, is a neurological disease that leads to paralysis. There is no cure, and the disease is 100 percent fatal. Because the respiratory muscles are affected, death usually occurs from slow suffocation. The illness gained national attention in 2014 when millions of people took part in the Ice Bucket Challenge to raise money for research. My husband's form of ALS mainly attacked the respiratory muscles, leading to bouts of pneumonia and severely compromised breathing. Unlike many other people with ALS, at the time of his death he retained some movements in his arms and legs.

My extended network of friends, neighbors, and family has been a true blessing. Thank you all for your help and kindness during John's extended illness. Following the death of my dad, husband, and only sibling in a horrific three-month period during the coldest, snowiest winter in decades, this network provided warm food, solace, and love. Members of my three writing groups have provided deep and honest feedback on many of the poems in this book.

Many deserve special thanks. Here you are, in no particular order:

Lesléa Newman, Jendi Reiter, Sally Bellerose, Oonagh Doherty, Lori Desrosiers, Mary Fister, Alex Risley-Schroeder, Charmagne Pruner, Gail Thomas, Becky Jones, Carolyn Cushing, Maria Williams, Erin Seibert, Michael Goldman, Mary Clare Powell, Howie Faerstein, Jan Lamberg, Barbara Sharp, Ginger Canton,

Karen Spindel, Kathryn Bayard Tracy, Kate Collins, Bill Hyland, Joe Tringali, Mary Vazquez, Brian Sheehy, Adam Cohen, Shelley Modell, and Krissy Park.

Staff at the Forbes Library provided technical and reference assistance as well as an aesthetically pleasing place to write, join poetry discussions, and share writing. I especially appreciate Benjamin Kalish, Molly Moss, Lisa Downing, Alene Moroni, Heather Diaz, and Julie Bartlett Nelson.

Many thanks to Ruth Thompson of Saddle Road Press for her skilled editorial eye and to Don Mitchell for his design skills. I appreciate all the work you both have done to bring this book to life.

Past writers in residence at the library, Diana Gordon, Susan Stinson and Naila Moreira, have enriched the local writing community by providing workshops, readings by local authors and weekly writing rooms.

My grandfather, Albert Beausoleil, kept my first poem, "The Sneezing Apron," folded in his wallet until the penciled words disintegrated. That poem is gone but his words of encouragement are with me still.

Special thanks to my late huband, John Clobridge, who during our hardest times never wavered in his love for me. He always believed.

My parents, Armand and Lorraine, worked hard and long in factories to help me get an education. You went above and beyond, thank you.

My beloved daughter Céline Vienneau has enriched my life beyond my deepest hopes. I couldn't ask for a more devoted or accomplished daughter.

Jeremy Vienneau is a kind and supportive son-in-law who became part of the in-home hospice team that cared for John in his final days. And thank you for your service as a veteran.

And most of all, I thank my beloved grandsons, Jackson and Zachary Vienneau, for the joy and laughter. I love you more than you can ever know.

Some of the poems in this book were published in print or online (occasionally with different titles).

"Credo for things that crack and break," in *Common Ground Review*; "The widow's dream sequence" (here, "Dream II"), "Lamentation for the 300th day without you," and "Prayer for the 542nd day without you" (here, "Benediction for the 364th unmarried day") in Cutthroat Journal (online); "Prayer for Weeping" (winner of the 2014 DASH Poetry Prize) in *DASH literary journal*; "The Stages of Loss," and "Prayer for the newlywed couple who bought our house after he died," in *Mudfish Journal*; "Blessing for an Imminent Death" (winner of the 2015 Joe Gouveia Outermost Poetry Prize), Outermost Poetry Contest website; "North into Fire," "All Souls" (published under title "Samhain"), and "We visit the cemetery where you might be buried," in the bilingual *Résonance Journal*; "Prayer for Despair," in Serving House Journal (online); "Before the sickness, when," "Quietly," "Because the dead cannot tell us what it's like to die," and "Prayer for the insanity of grief" (winner of the 2016 Robinson Jeffers Tor House Poetry Prize), in Tor House Poetry Website and newsletter; "After," "Things I lament," and "Fear, that good hallucinogen," at Writing in a Woman's Voice website.

About the Author

Ellen LaFlèche is the author of three chapbooks: *Workers' Rites* (Providence Athenaeum, 2011), *Ovarian* (Dallas Poets Community Press, 2011), and *Beatrice* (Tiger's Eye Press, 2013). She has published in diverse journals and websites, including *Hunger Mountain, The Ledge, Many Mountains Moving, Mudfish, Harpur Palate, Spoon River Poetry Review,* and *Naugatuck River Review.*

She is a recipient of the Ruth Stone Poetry Prize, the Tor House Poetry Prize, the Joe Gouveia Outermost Poetry Prize, the Philbrick Poetry Award, New Millennium Writings Poetry Award, and the Poets on Parnassus Prize for poetry about the medical experience, among others.

She lives in Northampton, Massachusetts, and is an assistant judge of the North Street Book Prize at Winningwriters.com.

CPSIA information can be obtained
at www.ICGtesting.com
Printed in the USA
LVHW090823290719
625691LV00003B/568/P

9 781732 952126